BACKYARD WILDLIFE

Beavers

by Emily Green

BELLWETHER MEDIA • MINNEAPOLIS, MN

Note to Librarians, Teachers, and Parents:

Blastoff! Readers are carefully developed by literacy experts and combine standards-based content with developmentally appropriate text.

Level 1 provides the most support through repetition of high-frequency words, light text, predictable sentence patterns, and strong visual support.

Level 2 offers early readers a bit more challenge through varied simple sentences, increased text load, and less repetition of high-frequency words.

Level 3 advances early-fluent readers toward fluency through increased text and concept load, less reliance on visuals, longer sentences, and more literary language.

Level 4 builds reading stamina by providing more text per page, increased use of punctuation, greater variation in sentence patterns, and increasingly challenging vocabulary.

Level 5 encourages children to move from "learning to read" to "reading to learn" by providing even more text, varied writing styles, and less familiar topics.

Whichever book is right for your reader, Blastoff! Readers are the perfect books to build confidence and encourage a love of reading that will last a lifetime!

This edition first published in 2011 by Bellwether Media, Inc.

No part of this publication may be reproduced in whole or in part without written permission of the publisher. For information regarding permission, write to Bellwether Media, Inc., Attention: Permissions Department, 5357 Penn Avenue South, Minneapolis, MN 55419.

Library of Congress Cataloging-in-Publication Data
Green, Emily K., 1966-
   Beavers / by Emily Green.
     p. cm. – (Backyard wildlife) (Blastoff! readers)
   Includes bibliographical references and index.
   Summary: "Developed by literacy experts for students in kindergarten through grade three, this book introduces beavers to young readers through leveled text and related photos"–Provided by publisher.
   ISBN 978-1-60014-560-5 (hardcover : alk. paper)
   1. Beavers–Juvenile literature. I. Title.
   QL737.R632G74 2011
   599.37–dc22   2010034531

Printed in the United States of America, North Mankato, MN.

010111   1176

Contents

Beavers are **rodents** with brown fur. They are great swimmers.

Beavers paddle through water with their long, flat tails and **webbed feet**.

Beavers eat plants and bark. They **gnaw** on bark with four long front teeth.

Beavers cut down trees with their front teeth. They use the wood to build **dams**.

Beavers also use mud and rocks to build dams. Dams control the flow of a river or stream.

Ponds form behind beaver dams. Beavers build **lodges** in these ponds.

lodge

pond

dam

Beavers live in the lodges. They enter them through underwater tunnels.

Lodges keep beavers safe from **predators**.

Beavers slap their tails on the water if they **sense** danger. Get inside the lodge!

Glossary

dams—piles of wood, mud, and rocks that beavers build to control the flow of a river or stream

gnaw—to bite or nibble on something for a long time

lodges—places where beavers live and sleep

ponds—small, shallow bodies of water; ponds often form behind beaver dams.

predators—animals that hunt other animals for food

rodents—a group of small animals that usually gnaw on their food

sense—to become aware of

webbed feet—feet with thin skin connecting the toes

To Learn More

AT THE LIBRARY

Kalman, Bobbie. *The Life Cycle of a Beaver.* New York, N.Y.: Crabtree Publishing, 2007.

MacDonald, Amy. *Little Beaver and the Echo.* New York, N.Y.: Putnam, 1990.

Vischer, Phil. *47 Beavers on the Big, Blue Sea.* Nashville, Tenn.: Tommy Nelson, 2007.

ON THE WEB

Learning more about beavers is as easy as 1, 2, 3.

1. Go to www.factsurfer.com.

2. Enter "beavers" into the search box.

3. Click the "Surf" button and you will see a list of related Web sites.

With factsurfer.com, finding more information is just a click away.

Index

The images in this book are reproduced through the courtesy of: Jack Milchanowski/Photolibrary, front cover; ARCO/H. Reinhard/Age Fotostock, p. 5; WILDLIFE GmbH/Alamy, p. 7; Reinhard/ARCO/naturepl.com, p. 7 (small); Donald M. Jones/Minden Pictures, p. 9; Kurt Madersbacher/Photolibrary, p. 9 (small); Tom & Pat Leeson/KimballStock, pp. 11, 19 (small), 21; Bernd Zoller/Photolibrary, p. 13; Arterra Picture Library/Alamy, p. 15; Konrad Wothe/Getty Images, p. 17; Picture Press/Alamy, p. 19.